The "French Slang Dictionary" is for anyone looking to immerse ever-evolving world of French : guide offers readers a deep  expressions and idiomatic phrases that characterize everyday French conversations. Unlike traditional dictionaries, this book focuses on the informal and often colorful language used by native speakers, providing insights into the cultural nuances and social contexts in which these expressions are used. Whether you're a student of French, a traveler, or simply a language enthusiast, this dictionary will enhance your understanding and appreciation of the French language.

Each entry in the "French Slang Dictionary" is meticulously curated to include not only the definition of the slang term but also examples of how it is used in real-life situations. The book is organized alphabetically, making it easy to navigate and find specific terms quickly.

The "French Slang Dictionary" is an essential addition to any language learner's library. Its thorough and engaging approach to slang makes it a valuable resource for achieving fluency and cultural literacy in French. Whether you're preparing for a trip to France, studying for an exam, or simply looking to broaden your linguistic horizons, this dictionary offers the tools you need to navigate the rich and varied world of French slang. With its clear explanations, extensive examples, and cultural context, the "French Slang Dictionary" is your key to mastering the informal and often playful side of the French language.

Index

A *3*

B *6*

C *9*

D *12*

E *15*

F *19*

G *22*

H *25*

I *28*

J *31*

K *34*

L *37*

M *40*

N *43*

O *46*

P *49*

Q *52*

R *55*

S *58*

T *61*

U 64

V 67

W 70

X 73

Y 76

Z.. 79

A

À l'arrache - On the fly, without preparation.

Example: "Il a fait son devoir à l'arrache." (He did his homework on the fly.)

Arnaque - Scam, fraud.

Example: "C'est une arnaque, ne l'achète pas." (It's a scam, don't buy it.)

Aperce - Aperitif.

Example: "On se prend un aperce ce soir?" (Shall we have an aperitif tonight?)

Avoir la dalle - To be very hungry.

Example: "J'ai la dalle, allons manger." (I'm starving, let's eat.)

Avoir le seum - To be annoyed or angry.

Example: "J'ai le seum contre lui." (I'm annoyed with him.)

Archi - Very, extremely.

Example: "C'était archi bien!" (It was extremely good!)

Avoine - Money.

Example: "Il a beaucoup d'avoine." (He has a lot of money.)

Arraché - High (on drugs).

Example: "Il était complètement arraché." (He was completely high.)

Ami(e) sûr(e) - Trusted friend.

Example: "C'est mon amie sûre." (She's my trusted friend.)

Avoir du bol - To be lucky.

Example: "Il a eu du bol de gagner." (He was lucky to win.)

Allô quoi! - Seriously! (Used to express disbelief).

Example: "Allô quoi! Tu plaisantes?" (Seriously! Are you kidding?)

Avoir un coup de barre - To feel suddenly tired.

Example: "Après le déjeuner, j'ai eu un coup de barre." (After lunch, I felt suddenly tired.)

Avoir la flemme - To be lazy.

Example: "J'ai la flemme de sortir." (I'm too lazy to go out.)

Avoir la patate - To feel great, energetic.

Example: "Aujourd'hui, j'ai la patate!" (Today, I feel great!)

À poil - Naked.

Example: "Il est sorti à poil." (He went out naked.)
Avoir un poil dans la main - To be lazy.

Example: "Il a un poil dans la main." (He is very lazy.)

Avoir la trouille - To be scared.

Example: "J'ai la trouille de parler en public." (I'm scared of public speaking.)

À donf - Full speed, very fast.

Example: "Il conduit toujours à donf." (He always drives very fast.)

Avoir du piston - To have connections.

Example: "Il a eu le job grâce à du piston." (He got the job thanks to connections.)

Avoir les boules - To be upset or frustrated.

Example: "J'ai les boules de perdre mon téléphone." (I'm upset about losing my phone.)

B

Bagnole - Car.

Example: "Ma bagnole est en panne." (My car broke down.)

Barjot - Crazy person.

Example: "Ce mec est un barjot." (That guy is crazy.)

Blé - Money.

Example: "Il a beaucoup de blé." (He has a lot of money.)

Bourré - Drunk.

Example: "Il est rentré bourré." (He came home drunk.)

Bobo - Small injury, boo-boo.

Example: "J'ai un petit bobo au doigt." (I have a small injury on my finger.)

Boulot - Job, work.

Example: "Je dois aller au boulot." (I have to go to work.)

Branché - Trendy, cool.

Example: "C'est un endroit très branché." (It's a very trendy place.)

Bidon - Fake, bogus.

Example: "Cette histoire est bidon." (This story is fake.)

Béton - Solid, reliable.

Example: "C'est un plan béton." (It's a solid plan.)

Bluffer - To bluff.

Example: "Il a essayé de me bluffer." (He tried to bluff me.)

Bardé - Loaded (with something).

Example: "Il est bardé de diplômes." (He is loaded with degrees.)

Barge - Crazy.

Example: "Elle est complètement barge." (She is completely crazy.)

Bac - High school diploma.

Example: "J'ai passé mon bac l'année dernière." (I took my high school diploma last year.)

Blague - Joke.

Example: "C'était une blague drôle." (It was a funny joke.)

Biche - Dear (term of endearment).

Example: "Comment ça va, ma biche?" (How are you, my dear?)

Bide - Flop, failure.

Example: "Le film a fait un bide." (The movie was a flop.)

Boulversé - Upset, shaken.

Example: "Il était boulversé par la nouvelle." (He was shaken by the news.)

Baraque - House, pad.

Example: "Il a une grande baraque." (He has a big house.)

Blasé - Indifferent, unimpressed.

Example: "Il est blasé de tout." (He is indifferent to everything.)

Bobo - Hipster.

Example: "Le quartier est plein de bobos." (The neighborhood is full of hipsters.)

C

Caisse - Car.

Example: "J'ai une nouvelle caisse." (I have a new car.)

Clope - Cigarette.

Example: "Tu as une clope?" (Do you have a cigarette?)

C'est clair - It's clear, obviously.

Example: "C'est clair qu'il va pleuvoir." (It's clear that it's going to rain.)

C'est ouf - That's crazy.

Example: "C'est ouf ce qui s'est passé." (What happened is crazy.)

Chiant - Annoying.

Example: "Ce travail est chiant." (This job is annoying.)

C'est du lourd - It's awesome.

Example: "Ce film, c'est du lourd." (This movie is awesome.)

Craquer - To lose it, to break down.

Example: "Il a craqué après la réunion." (He lost it after the meeting.)

Charrier - To tease, to mock.

Example: "Il aime charrier ses amis." (He likes to tease his friends.)

Cinglé - Crazy, nuts.

Example: "Ce type est complètement cinglé." (That guy is completely nuts.)

C'est top - It's great.

Example: "Ton idée, c'est top!" (Your idea is great!)

Carton - Success, hit.

Example: "Le concert a fait un carton." (The concert was a hit.)

Casser les pieds - To annoy, to bother.

Example: "Tu me casses les pieds!" (You're bothering me!)

Cafter - To snitch.

Example: "Ne cafte pas ce que je t'ai dit." (Don't snitch on what I told you.)

C'est de la balle - It's awesome.

Example: "Cette fête, c'est de la balle!" (This party is awesome!)

Choper - To catch, to get.

Example: "Il a chopé un rhume." (He caught a cold.)

C'est clair et net - It's clear and obvious.

Example: "C'est clair et net qu'il ment." (It's clear and obvious that he's lying.)

Craignos - Shady, sketchy.

Example: "Ce quartier est un peu craignos." (This neighborhood is a bit shady.)

Cramer - To burn, to get caught.

Example: "Il s'est fait cramer en train de tricher." (He got caught cheating.)

Causer - To talk.

Example: "On peut causer après le travail?" (Can we talk after work?)

Casser la croûte - To have a meal.

Example: "On va casser la croûte ensemble?" (Shall we have a meal together?)

D

Débile - Stupid, idiotic.

Example: "Ce film est débile." (This movie is stupid.)

Dégueu - Disgusting.

Example: "Ce plat est dégueu." (This dish is disgusting.)

Drague - Flirting.

Example: "Il est toujours en train de draguer." (He's always flirting.)

Daron - Dad.

Example: "Mon daron est cool." (My dad is cool.)

Déconner - To joke, to mess around.

Example: "Arrête de déconner!" (Stop joking around!)

Dodo - Sleep.

Example: "Il est temps de faire dodo." (It's time to sleep.)

Débarquer - To arrive unexpectedly.

Example: "Il a débarqué chez moi." (He arrived at my place unexpectedly.)

Défoncé - High, wasted.

Example: "Il était complètement défoncé." (He was completely high.)

Dégager - To leave, to get out.

Example: "Dégage d'ici!" (Get out of here!)

Déboussolé - Confused, disoriented.

Example: "Il est déboussolé après la nouvelle." (He is confused after the news.)

Dégoter - To find, to get.

Example: "J'ai dégotté un super appart." (I found a great apartment.)

Déjanté - Crazy, wild.

Example: "Cette soirée était déjantée." (This party was wild.)

Déprimé - Depressed.

Example: "Il est déprimé depuis son divorce." (He has been depressed since his divorce.)

Déglingué - Broken, messed up.

Example: "Mon vélo est déglingué." (My bike is broken.)
Dégoûté - Disgusted.

Example: "Je suis dégoûté par son comportement." (I am disgusted by his behavior.)

Dingue - Crazy.

Example: "C'est dingue cette histoire!" (This story is crazy!)

Démarrer - To start.

Example: "Il faut démarrer tôt demain." (We need to start early tomorrow.)

Déraper - To slip, to go out of control.

Example: "La situation a dérapé." (The situation went out of control.)

Déçu - Disappointed.

Example: "Je suis déçu par le résultat." (I am disappointed with the result.)

Délirer - To be crazy, to talk nonsense.

Example: "Il délire complètement." (He is talking nonsense.)

E

Éclater - To have fun.

Example: "On s'est éclatés à la fête." (We had fun at the party.)

Énervé - Angry.

Example: "Il est très énervé aujourd'hui." (He is very angry today.)

Embrouille - Conflict, trouble.

Example: "Il y a eu une embrouille au travail." (There was a conflict at work.)

En galère - In trouble.

Example: "Je suis en galère avec ce projet." (I'm in trouble with this project.)

Épater - To impress.

Example: "Il m'a épaté avec ses talents." (He impressed me with his talents.)

Escroc - Crook, swindler.

Example: "Ce type est un escroc." (That guy is a crook.)

Épuisé - Exhausted.

Example: "Je suis épuisé après cette journée." (I am exhausted after this day.)

Éclater de rire - To burst out laughing.

Example: "On a éclaté de rire en entendant la blague." (We burst out laughing when we heard the joke.)

En avoir marre - To be fed up.

Example: "J'en ai marre de cette situation." (I am fed up with this situation.)

Épauler - To support.

Example: "Il m'a épaulé pendant le projet." (He supported me during the project.)

Être à la bourre - To be late.

Example: "Je suis à la bourre pour le rendez-vous." (I am late for the appointment.)

Énorme - Awesome, great.

Example: "Ce concert était énorme!" (This concert was awesome!)

Énergumène - Eccentric person.

Example: "Cet énergumène fait toujours des choses bizarres." (This eccentric person always does strange things.)

Éclabousser - To splash.

Example: "La voiture m'a éclaboussé." (The car splashed me.)

Épatant - Amazing.

Example: "C'est un spectacle épatant!" (It's an amazing show!)

Embêter - To bother.

Example: "Ne m'embête pas maintenant." (Don't bother me now.)

Égaré - Lost.

Example: "Je me suis égaré en route." (I got lost on the way.)

Embrouillé - Confused.

Example: "Je suis embrouillé avec toutes ces informations." (I am confused with all this information.)

Économe - Thrifty.

Example: "Il est très économe avec son argent." (He is very thrifty with his money.)

Éclopé - Injured, crippled.

Example: "Il est éclopé après l'accident." (He is injured after the accident.)

F

Flic - Cop.

Example: "Les flics sont arrivés rapidement." (The cops arrived quickly.)

Flouze - Money.

Example: "Il a beaucoup de flouze." (He has a lot of money.)

Fauché - Broke, without money.

Example: "Je suis fauché ce mois-ci." (I am broke this month.)

Fête - Party.

Example: "On va à une fête ce soir." (We're going to a party tonight.)

Frangin - Brother.

Example: "Mon frangin vient ce week-end." (My brother is coming this weekend.)

Flemme - Laziness.

Example: "J'ai la flemme de travailler." (I am too lazy to work.)

Fou - Crazy.

Example: "Il est fou ce mec!" (That guy is crazy!)

Frimer - To show off.

Example: "Il aime frimer avec sa voiture." (He likes to show off with his car.)

Flipper - To freak out.

Example: "J'ai flippé pendant le film." (I freaked out during the movie.)

Foirer - To mess up.

Example: "Il a foiré son examen." (He messed up his exam.)

Foutre - To do, to put (vulgar).

Example: "Qu'est-ce que tu fous?" (What are you doing?)

Filon - Opportunity, good deal.

Example: "J'ai trouvé un bon filon." (I found a good deal.)

Fayot - Suck-up, teacher's pet.

Example: "Il est toujours en train de fayoter." (He's always sucking up.)

Fiston - Son.

Example: "Mon fiston a grandi." (My son has grown up.)

Flingue - Gun.

Example: "Il a sorti un flingue." (He pulled out a gun.)

Frousse - Fear.

Example: "J'ai eu la frousse de ma vie." (I was scared to death.)

Fringues - Clothes.

Example: "J'aime tes fringues." (I like your clothes.)

Faire gaffe - To be careful.

Example: "Fais gaffe en traversant la rue." (Be careful crossing the street.)

Faire la gueule - To sulk.

Example: "Il fait la gueule depuis hier." (He's been sulking since yesterday.)

Fric - Money.

Example: "Il a beaucoup de fric." (He has a lot of money.)

G

Gosse - Kid.

Example: "Il a deux gosses." (He has two kids.)

Glander - To laze around.

Example: "Il passe son temps à glander." (He spends his time lazing around.)

Gueule - Mouth, face.

Example: "Ferme ta gueule!" (Shut your mouth!)

Galère - Trouble, struggle.

Example: "C'est la galère en ce moment." (It's a struggle right now.)

Gratter - To get for free.

Example: "Il aime gratter des trucs gratuits." (He likes to get free stuff.)

Gaffe - Mistake, blunder.

Example: "J'ai fait une gaffe." (I made a mistake.)

Goujat - Rude person.

Example: "Quel goujat!" (What a rude person!)

Gueuler - To shout.

Example: "Il a commencé à gueuler." (He started shouting.)

Gober - To believe (naively).

Example: "Il gobe tout ce qu'on lui dit." (He believes everything he's told.)

Génial - Great, awesome.

Example: "Ce film est génial!" (This movie is great!)

Gigoter - To fidget.

Example: "Il n'arrête pas de gigoter." (He can't stop fidgeting.)

Grailler - To eat.

Example: "On va grailler ce soir?" (Shall we eat tonight?)

Gringalet - Weak, skinny person.

Example: "C'est un gringalet." (He is a weak person.)

Gonzesse - Woman (informal).

Example: "Il sort avec une nouvelle gonzesse." (He's dating a new woman.)

Gueule de bois - Hangover.

Example: "J'ai une gueule de bois ce matin." (I have a hangover this morning.)

Gober - To swallow.

Example: "Il a gobé le bonbon." (He swallowed the candy.)

Gosse - Child.

Example: "Elle a trois gosses." (She has three children.)

Gaver - To annoy, to bore.

Example: "Ça me gave!" (That annoys me!)

Gratter - To scratch.

Example: "Il a gratté son billet de loterie." (He scratched his lottery ticket.)

Grave - Seriously, very.

Example: "C'est grave cool ici." (It's very cool here.)

H

Hallu - Hallucination.

Example: "J'ai eu une hallu en voyant ça." (I had a hallucination seeing that.)

Hargne - Aggressiveness.

Example: "Il a répondu avec hargne." (He responded aggressively.)

Harceler - To harass.

Example: "Il ne cesse de m'harceler." (He keeps harassing me.)

Hélico - Helicopter.

Example: "Un hélico a survolé la ville." (A helicopter flew over the city.)

Hallucinant - Incredible, unbelievable.

Example: "C'est hallucinant ce qu'il a fait!" (What he did is unbelievable!)

Héberger - To host, to accommodate.

Example: "Il m'a hébergé chez lui." (He hosted me at his place.)

Hypé - Hyped, excited.

Example: "Je suis trop hypé pour le concert." (I'm so hyped for the concert.)

Hardi - Bold, daring.

Example: "C'est un gars hardi." (He's a bold guy.)

Heureux - Happy.

Example: "Il est heureux de sa réussite." (He is happy with his success.)

Hoche - Nod.

Example: "Il a hoché la tête en signe d'accord." (He nodded in agreement.)

Humer - To smell, to sniff.

Example: "Il a humé l'air frais." (He sniffed the fresh air.)

Habile - Skillful.

Example: "Il est très habile de ses mains." (He is very skillful with his hands.)

Honte - Shame.

Example: "Il a honte de son comportement." (He is ashamed of his behavior.)

Hirsute - Shaggy, disheveled.

Example: "Il est toujours hirsute le matin." (He is always disheveled in the morning.)

Huer - To boo.

Example: "Le public a hué le chanteur." (The audience booed the singer.)

Hargneux - Aggressive.

Example: "Il est devenu hargneux." (He became aggressive.)

Hymne - Anthem.

Example: "Ils ont chanté l'hymne national." (They sang the national anthem.)

Hurler - To scream.

Example: "Elle a hurlé de peur." (She screamed in fear.)

Houleux - Stormy, rough.

Example: "Le débat était houleux." (The debate was rough.)

Haleter - To pant.

Example: "Il haletait après la course." (He was panting after the race.)

I

Impec - Perfect.

Example: "Tout est impec!" (Everything is perfect!)

Ivre - Drunk.

Example: "Il est rentré ivre hier soir." (He came home drunk last night.)

Inquiétant - Worrying.

Example: "C'est un signe inquiétant." (That's a worrying sign.)

Ingénu - Naive, innocent.

Example: "C'est un garçon ingénu." (He's a naive boy.)

Inouï - Unheard of, incredible.

Example: "C'est inouï ce qu'il a fait!" (What he did is incredible!)

Imbroglio - Confusion, mess.

Example: "L'affaire est un vrai imbroglio." (The matter is a real mess.)

Intrépide - Fearless.

Example: "C'est un aventurier intrépide." (He's a fearless adventurer.)

Irréprochable - Blameless, perfect.

Example: "Son travail est irréprochable." (His work is blameless.)

Insensé - Insane, crazy.

Example: "C'est une idée insensée." (That's a crazy idea.)

Insipide - Tasteless, bland.

Example: "La soupe est insipide." (The soup is bland.)

Insolent - Insolent, cheeky.

Example: "Il a un comportement insolent." (He has a cheeky behavior.)

Inoxydable - Unbreakable, reliable.

Example: "Il est inoxydable dans son domaine." (He is unbreakable in his field.)

Inculte - Uneducated, uncultured.

Example: "Il est complètement inculte." (He is completely uneducated.)

Ingérable - Unmanageable.

Example: "Cette situation est ingérable." (This situation is unmanageable.)

Intox - Disinformation.

Example: "Ne crois pas à cette intox." (Don't believe that disinformation.)

Inespéré - Unhoped-for, unexpected.

Example: "C'est un succès inespéré." (It's an unexpected success.)

Incruster - To embed, to stick around (uninvited).

Example: "Il s'est incrusté à la fête." (He stuck around at the party uninvited.)

Impérissable - Everlasting.

Example: "Un souvenir impérissable." (An everlasting memory.)

Insolite - Unusual.

Example: "Un événement insolite." (An unusual event.)

Infructueux - Unsuccessful.

Example: "La recherche a été infructueuse." (The search was unsuccessful.)

J

Jacter - To chat, to talk.

Example: "Ils n'arrêtent pas de jacter." (They keep talking.)

Jeunot - Youngster.

Example: "C'est un jeunot dans le métier." (He's a youngster in the job.)

Jouissif - Pleasurable, enjoyable.

Example: "C'était un moment jouissif." (It was an enjoyable moment.)

Jacasser - To chatter.

Example: "Elle jacasse toute la journée." (She chatters all day long.)

Jauge - Capacity, gauge.

Example: "La jauge est pleine." (The gauge is full.)

Joli - Pretty, nice.

Example: "Quel joli cadeau!" (What a nice gift!)

Jovial - Cheerful.

Example: "Il a un caractère jovial." (He has a cheerful character.)

Jongler - To juggle.

Example: "Il sait jongler avec les responsabilités." (He knows how to juggle responsibilities.)

Jouer la comédie - To act, to pretend.

Example: "Il joue la comédie pour obtenir ce qu'il veut." (He acts to get what he wants.)

Jubilant - Jubilant, exultant.

Example: "Elle était jubilante après sa victoire." (She was jubilant after her victory.)

Jaunir - To turn yellow.

Example: "Les feuilles commencent à jaunir." (The leaves are starting to turn yellow.)

Jucher - To perch.

Example: "L'oiseau est juché sur la branche." (The bird is perched on the branch.)

Juteux - Juicy.

Example: "Un fruit juteux." (A juicy fruit.)

Jubilé - Jubilee, celebration.

Example: "Ils ont célébré leur jubilé." (They celebrated their jubilee.)

Jauge - Measure, to gauge.

Example: "Il faut jauger la situation." (We need to gauge the situation.)

Javel - Bleach.

Example: "Il a utilisé de la javel pour nettoyer." (He used bleach to clean.)

Jouir - To enjoy, to take pleasure.

Example: "Elle sait jouir de la vie." (She knows how to enjoy life.)

Javelliser - To bleach.

Example: "Il a javellisé le linge." (He bleached the laundry.)

Joncher - To litter, to cover.

Example: "Les feuilles jonchent le sol." (The leaves litter the ground.)

Joujou - Toy.

Example: "L'enfant adore son joujou." (The child loves his toy.)

K

Kiffer - To like, to enjoy.

Example: "Je kiffe cette chanson." (I like this song.)

Kif-kif - Same, equal.

Example: "C'est kif-kif pour moi." (It's the same for me.)

Kéké - Show-off.

Example: "Il fait son kéké avec sa nouvelle voiture." (He's showing off with his new car.)

Kilos - Pounds (weight).

Example: "Il a perdu quelques kilos." (He lost a few pounds.)

Karaoké - Karaoke.

Example: "On va au karaoké ce soir." (We're going to karaoke tonight.)

Kitch - Tacky, gaudy.

Example: "Ce style est un peu kitch." (This style is a bit tacky.)

Kick - Kick.

Example: "Il a donné un kick au ballon." (He kicked the ball.)

Kérosène - Jet fuel.

Example: "L'avion a besoin de kérosène." (The plane needs jet fuel.)

Krach - Crash (financial).

Example: "Il y a eu un krach boursier." (There was a stock market crash.)

Klaxon - Horn (car).

Example: "Il a klaxonné pour avertir." (He honked to warn.)

Kiwi - Kiwi (fruit).

Example: "Le kiwi est riche en vitamines." (Kiwi is rich in vitamins.)

Kabyle - Kabyle (ethnic group).

Example: "Il est d'origine kabyle." (He is of Kabyle origin.)

Kermesse - Fair, festival.

Example: "La kermesse de l'école est demain." (The school fair is tomorrow.)

Koala - Koala.

Example: "Les koalas vivent en Australie." (Koalas live in Australia.)

Kara - Carat (weight of gems).

Example: "Un diamant de plusieurs karats." (A diamond of several carats.)

Karaté - Karate.

Example: "Il pratique le karaté." (He practices karate.)

Kyst - Cyst.

Example: "Il doit se faire enlever un kyste." (He has to have a cyst removed.)

Kermesse - Bazaar.

Example: "Ils ont organisé une kermesse." (They organized a bazaar.)

Kimono - Kimono.

Example: "Elle a acheté un kimono japonais." (She bought a Japanese kimono.)

Kilt - Kilt.

Example: "Le kilt est un vêtement traditionnel écossais." (The kilt is a traditional Scottish garment.)

L

Louper - To miss.

Example: "J'ai loupé mon bus." (I missed my bus.)

Laisse béton - Forget it.

Example: "Laisse béton, c'est pas grave." (Forget it, it's not important.)

Lèche - To suck up.

Example: "Il lèche toujours les bottes du patron." (He's always sucking up to the boss.)

Lourd - Heavy, annoying.

Example: "Il est lourd avec ses blagues." (He's annoying with his jokes.)

Loulou - Sweetie, darling.

Example: "Viens ici, mon loulou." (Come here, my sweetie.)

Larbin - Servant, lackey.

Example: "Il se comporte comme un larbin." (He acts like a lackey.)

Loufoque - Crazy, zany.

Example: "Ce film est loufoque." (This movie is zany.

Lèche-vitrine - Window shopping.

Example: "Elle adore faire du lèche-vitrine." (She loves window shopping.)

Loubard - Hoodlum.

Example: "C'est un loubard de quartier." (He's a neighborhood hoodlum.)

Limer - To file.

Example: "Il faut limer les ongles." (You need to file your nails.)

Laitier - Milkman.

Example: "Le laitier passe tous les matins." (The milkman comes every morning.)

Larve - Slug, lazy person.

Example: "Il passe ses journées comme une larve." (He spends his days like a slug.)

Lèche-cul - Brown-noser.

Example: "C'est un vrai lèche-cul." (He's a real brown-noser.)

Langue de vipère - Gossip, malicious talker.

Example: "Elle a une langue de vipère." (She's a malicious talker.)

Lardon - Bacon bit.

Example: "Ajoute des lardons à la salade." (Add bacon bits to the salad.)

Lassé - Bored, tired.

Example: "Je suis lassé de cette routine." (I am bored of this routine.)

Leurre - Deception, decoy.

Example: "C'est un leurre pour nous tromper." (It's a decoy to deceive us.)

Louange - Praise.

Example: "Il a reçu des louanges pour son travail." (He received praise for his work.)

Libidineux - Lustful.

Example: "Il a un regard libidineux." (He has a lustful look.)

Lugubre - Gloomy.

Example: "Le cimetière est lugubre la nuit." (The cemetery is gloomy at night.)

M

Mec - Guy.

Example: "C'est un mec sympa." (He's a nice guy.)

Moche - Ugly.

Example: "Ce pull est moche." (This sweater is ugly.)

Merde - Shit.

Example: "Oh merde, j'ai oublié!" (Oh shit, I forgot!)

Mortel - Awesome, deadly.

Example: "Ce concert était mortel!" (This concert was awesome!)

Marrant - Funny.

Example: "Ce film est marrant." (This movie is funny.)

Magouille - Scam.

Example: "C'est une magouille politique." (It's a political scam.)

Môme - Kid.

Example: "Il a deux mômes." (He has two kids.)

Manouche - Gypsy.

Example: "Il vit comme un manouche." (He lives like a gypsy.)

Mastard - Big, strong person.

Example: "C'est un vrai mastard." (He's a really big guy.)

Moule - Mussel, lucky person.

Example: "Il a eu de la moule." (He was lucky.)

Malin - Clever.

Example: "Il est malin comme un singe." (He's as clever as a monkey.)

Méchant - Mean, bad.

Example: "Il est méchant avec ses amis." (He's mean to his friends.)

Minable - Pathetic.

Example: "Son excuse était minable." (His excuse was pathetic.)

Magot - Stash of money.

Example: "Il a un magot caché." (He has a hidden stash of money.)

Mamie - Grandma.

Example: "J'aime aller chez ma mamie." (I love going to my grandma's house.)

Moisi - Moldy.

Example: "Le pain est tout moisi." (The bread is all moldy.)

Monture - Mount (horse), frames (glasses).

Example: "J'aime bien ta monture de lunettes." (I like your glasses' frames.)

Mufle - Boor, lout.

Example: "Quel mufle!" (What a boor!)

Moulin - Windmill, talkative person.

Example: "Elle est un vrai moulin à paroles." (She's a real chatterbox.)

Morfler - To suffer, to get hit.

Example: "Il a morflé pendant l'entraînement." (He suffered during the training.)

N

Nana - Girl.

Example: "Il sort avec une nouvelle nana." (He's dating a new girl.)

Naze - Lame, stupid.

Example: "Ce film est naze." (This movie is lame.)

Narguer - To mock, to taunt.

Example: "Il n'arrête pas de me narguer." (He keeps mocking me.)

Navet - Turnip, flop (bad movie).

Example: "Ce film est un vrai navet." (This movie is a real flop.)

Niaiserie - Foolishness.

Example: "Arrête avec tes niaiseries!" (Stop with your foolishness!)

Nouille - Noodle, idiot.

Example: "Il est bête comme une nouille." (He's as dumb as a noodle.)

Noyer - To drown.

Example: "Il a failli se noyer." (He almost drowned.)

Nostalgique - Nostalgic.

Example: "Elle est nostalgique de son enfance." (She is nostalgic for her childhood.)

Nif - Nose.

Example: "Il a un grand nif." (He has a big nose.)

Naze - Broken, exhausted.

Example: "Je suis complètement naze." (I am completely exhausted.)

Nain - Dwarf.

Example: "Il ressemble à un nain." (He looks like a dwarf.)

Nigaud - Simpleton.

Example: "Il est vraiment nigaud." (He's really a simpleton.)

Navrant - Deplorable.

Example: "C'est navrant de voir ça." (It's deplorable to see that.)

Nouba - Party.

Example: "Ils ont fait la nouba toute la nuit." (They partied all night.)

Nanar - B-movie, bad film.

Example: "Ce film est un nanar." (This film is a B-movie.)

Nasse - Trap.

Example: "Il est tombé dans une nasse." (He fell into a trap.)

Népote - Nephew, grandchild.

Example: "C'est mon népote préféré." (He's my favorite grandchild.)

Néant - Nothingness, void.

Example: "Il parle du néant." (He's talking about nothingness.)

Nuit blanche - Sleepless night.

Example: "J'ai passé une nuit blanche." (I had a sleepless night.)

Nouvelle vague - New wave.

Example: "C'est un film de la nouvelle vague." (It's a new wave film.)

O

Oseille - Money.

Example: "Il a plein d'oseille." (He has a lot of money.)

Ouf - Crazy.

Example: "Ce mec est ouf." (This guy is crazy.)

Ok - Okay.

Example: "C'est ok pour moi." (It's okay for me.)

Os - Bone.

Example: "Il a cassé un os." (He broke a bone.)

Ouistiti - Marmoset, used to make someone smile in photos.

Example: "Dis ouistiti!" (Say cheese!)

Onglet - Tab, steak cut.

Example: "J'ai ouvert un nouvel onglet." (I opened a new tab.)

Otarie - Sea lion.

Example: "Les otaries sont amusantes." (Sea lions are fun.)

Opinel - Type of knife.

Example: "Il a un opinel dans sa poche." (He has an Opinel knife in his pocket.)

Olé - Exclamation of approval.

Example: "Olé! Bravo!" (Olé! Well done!)

Olibrius - Eccentric person.

Example: "C'est un drôle d'olibrius." (He's a funny eccentric.)

Ouf - Phew, relief.

Example: "Ouf, on a réussi." (Phew, we made it.)

Oseille - Sorrel (plant).

Example: "L'oseille pousse bien ici." (Sorrel grows well here.)

Or - Gold.

Example: "Ce bijou est en or." (This jewel is made of gold.)

Odeur - Smell.

Example: "Quelle odeur agréable!" (What a pleasant smell!)

Ordure - Trash, scumbag.

Example: "C'est une ordure." (He's a scumbag.)

Obus - Shell (artillery).

Example: "Un obus a explosé." (A shell exploded.)

Orage - Storm.

Example: "Il y a un orage ce soir." (There's a storm tonight.)

Oeil-de-boeuf - Small round window.

Example: "La maison a un oeil-de-boeuf." (The house has a small round window.)

Ouragan - Hurricane.

Example: "Un ouragan approche." (A hurricane is approaching.)

Onduler - To wave, to undulate.

Example: "Les rideaux ondulent au vent." (The curtains wave in the wind.)

P

Pote - Buddy.

Example: "C'est mon pote." (He's my buddy.)

Piger - To understand.

Example: "Tu piges ce que je dis?" (Do you understand what I'm saying?)

Plouc - Hick, redneck.

Example: "Il se comporte comme un plouc." (He behaves like a hick.)

Pif - Nose.

Example: "Il a un gros pif." (He has a big nose.)

Pépère - Comfortable, easygoing.

Example: "Il mène une vie pépère." (He leads an easygoing life.)

Poubelle - Trash can.

Example: "Jette ça à la poubelle." (Throw that in the trash can.)

Péter - To fart, to break.

Example: "Il a pété une vitre." (He broke a window.)

Pâlot - Pale.

Example: "Il a l'air pâlot." (He looks pale.)

Pinard - Wine.

Example: "On boit du pinard ce soir." (We're drinking wine tonight.)

Pied - Foot.

Example: "J'ai mal au pied." (My foot hurts.)

Paumé - Lost, isolated.

Example: "Il vit dans un village paumé." (He lives in a remote village.)

Paresseux - Lazy.

Example: "Il est très paresseux." (He's very lazy.)

Pétard - Firecracker, joint.

Example: "Ils ont fait péter des pétards." (They set off firecrackers.)

Puce - Flea, chip.

Example: "Mon chien a des puces." (My dog has fleas.)

Plafond - Ceiling.

Example: "Le plafond est haut." (The ceiling is high.)

Plaisantin - Joker, prankster.

Example: "C'est un vrai plaisantin." (He's a real joker.)

Plume - Feather, pen.

Example: "Il a trouvé une plume d'oiseau." (He found a bird's feather.)

Plein - Full.

Example: "Le verre est plein." (The glass is full.)

Pénible - Annoying, difficult.

Example: "Ce travail est pénible." (This job is difficult.)

Peur bleue - Terrified.

Example: "J'ai eu une peur bleue." (I was terrified.)

Q

Que dalle - Nothing.

Example: "J'ai reçu que dalle." (I got nothing.)

Quiche - Fool, silly person.

Example: "Il est vraiment quiche." (He's really silly.)

Québlo - Stuck.

Example: "Je suis québlo dans les embouteillages." (I'm stuck in traffic.)

QG - Headquarters.

Example: "Le QG est à Paris." (The headquarters are in Paris.)

Queue - Tail, line.

Example: "Il y a une longue queue." (There's a long line.)

Quenotte - Little tooth.

Example: "Le bébé a une quenotte." (The baby has a little tooth.)

Quartier - Neighborhood.

Example: "C'est un quartier calme." (It's a quiet neighborhood.)

Quotidien - Daily.

Example: "C'est son rituel quotidien." (It's his daily ritual.)

Quitte - Even, free from debt.

Example: "Nous sommes quittes." (We are even.)

Quasi - Almost, nearly.

Example: "Il est quasi prêt." (He's almost ready.)

Querelle - Quarrel.

Example: "Ils ont une querelle." (They have a quarrel.)

Queue de poisson - Abrupt ending.

Example: "L'histoire se termine en queue de poisson." (The story ends abruptly.)

Quiproquo - Misunderstanding.

Example: "C'était un quiproquo." (It was a misunderstanding.)

Quincaillerie - Hardware store.

Example: "Il travaille dans une quincaillerie." (He works in a hardware store.)

Quiche - Savory pie.

Example: "J'ai préparé une quiche pour le dîner." (I made a quiche for dinner.)

Quadriller - To grid, to patrol.

Example: "La police quadrille la zone." (The police are patrolling the area.)

Quintal - Quintal (metric weight).

Example: "Il a vendu un quintal de blé." (He sold a quintal of wheat.)

Quête - Quest, search.

Example: "Ils sont en quête de vérité." (They are on a quest for truth.)

Quotité - Portion, share.

Example: "Sa quotité est définie par le contrat." (His portion is defined by the contract.)

Quidam - Anonymous person.

Example: "Un quidam est passé par là." (An anonymous person passed by.)

R

Radin - Stingy.

Example: "Il est trop radin pour payer." (He's too stingy to pay.)

Ras-le-bol - Fed up.

Example: "J'en ai ras-le-bol!" (I'm fed up!)

Rigo - Funny.

Example: "Ce mec est rigo." (This guy is funny.)

Rouler - To roll, to drive.

Example: "Il roule en voiture." (He's driving.)

Râteau - Rake, rejection.

Example: "Il a pris un râteau." (He got rejected.)

Raté - Failed.

Example: "Le gâteau est raté." (The cake is failed.)

Râler - To grumble.

Example: "Il râle tout le temps." (He grumbles all the time.)

Rififi - Trouble, fight.

Example: "Il y a eu du rififi hier soir." (There was trouble last night.)

Roublard - Cunning, sly.

Example: "Il est roublard." (He's cunning.)

Roulotte - Caravan.

Example: "Ils vivent dans une roulotte." (They live in a caravan.)

Relou - Annoying, tiresome.

Example: "C'est vraiment relou." (That's really annoying.)

Rembarrer - To snub.

Example: "Il m'a rembarré." (He snubbed me.)

Rigoler - To laugh.

Example: "On a bien rigolé." (We had a good laugh.)

Ramdam - Ruckus, commotion.

Example: "Quel ramdam!" (What a commotion!)

Réglo - Honest, fair.

Example: "Il est réglo." (He's honest.)

Rab - Extra, more.

Example: "Je veux du rab." (I want more.)

Roupiller - To sleep.

Example: "Il roupille encore." (He's still sleeping.)

Radin - Stingy.

Example: "Il est trop radin pour partager." (He's too stingy to share.)

Rasoir - Boring.

Example: "Ce film est rasoir." (This movie is boring.)

Rasé - Shaved.

Example: "Il s'est rasé la barbe." (He shaved his beard.)

S

Sapeur - Dandy, stylish dresser.

Example: "Il est un vrai sapeur." (He's a real dandy.)

Seum - Frustration.

Example: "J'ai le seum." (I'm frustrated.)

Squatter - To squat, to crash.

Example: "Il squat chez moi ce soir." (He's crashing at my place tonight.)

Surfer - To surf (internet).

Example: "Je surfe sur le net." (I'm surfing the web.)

S'enjailler - To have fun.

Example: "On va s'enjailler ce soir." (We're going to have fun tonight.)

Sympa - Nice, friendly.

Example: "Ce mec est sympa." (This guy is nice.)

Sérieux - Seriously.

Example: "Sérieux?!" (Seriously?!)

Soudoyer - To bribe.

Example: "Il a soudoyé le garde." (He bribed the guard.)

Sans-gêne - Shameless.

Example: "Elle est sans-gêne." (She is shameless.)

Saper - To undermine.

Example: "Il a sapé mon autorité." (He undermined my authority.)

Saperlipopette - Gosh, good heavens.

Example: "Saperlipopette, c'est incroyable!" (Gosh, that's incredible!)

Scotché - Glued, amazed.

Example: "J'étais scotché par la nouvelle." (I was amazed by the news.)

Schlinguer - To stink.

Example: "Ça schlingue ici." (It stinks here.)

Se taper - To have sex.

Example: "Il s'est tapé une fille." (He had sex with a girl.)

Saccager - To vandalize.

Example: "Ils ont saccagé le parc." (They vandalized the park.)

Se vautrer - To sprawl, to fail.

Example: "Il s'est vautré par terre." (He sprawled on the ground.)

Salopard - Bastard, scumbag.

Example: "C'est un vrai salopard." (He's a real bastard.)

S'enfuir - To flee.

Example: "Ils se sont enfuis." (They fled.)

S'occuper - To take care of.

Example: "Je m'occupe de ça." (I'm taking care of that.)

Se barrer - To leave, to split.

Example: "Il s'est barré." (He left.)

T

Truc - Thing.

Example: "C'est quoi ce truc?" (What's this thing?)

Trop - Too much, very.

Example: "C'est trop bien!" (It's really good!)

Taf - Work, job.

Example: "J'ai du taf." (I have work.)

Toc - Fake, knock.

Example: "Ce sac est en toc." (This bag is fake.)

Tordu - Twisted, crazy.

Example: "C'est un plan tordu." (It's a twisted plan.)

Taffer - To work.

Example: "Je taffe jusqu'à tard." (I work until late.)

Tard - Late.

Example: "Il est trop tard." (It's too late.)

Teuf - Party.

Example: "On va à une teuf ce soir." (We're going to a party tonight.)

Tocard - Loser.

Example: "C'est un tocard." (He's a loser.)

Tombé - Fallen.

Example: "Il est tombé amoureux." (He fell in love.)

Taré - Crazy.

Example: "Il est complètement taré." (He's completely crazy.)

Tanguer - To sway.

Example: "Le bateau tangue." (The boat is swaying.)

Tordu - Crooked, twisted.

Example: "Le chemin est tordu." (The path is crooked.)

Trempé - Soaked.

Example: "Je suis trempé." (I'm soaked.)

Toc-toc - Knock-knock, silly.

Example: "Il est un peu toc-toc." (He's a bit silly.)

Tressé - Braided.

Example: "Ses cheveux sont tressés." (Her hair is braided.)

Tordu - Devious, cunning.

Example: "C'est un plan tordu." (It's a devious plan.)

Toujours - Always.

Example: "Il est toujours en retard." (He's always late.)

Terrible - Terrible, awesome.

Example: "Ce film est terrible." (This movie is awesome.)

Tracasser - To worry.

Example: "Ça me tracasse." (It worries me.)

U

Usé - Worn out.

Example: "Mes chaussures sont usées." (My shoes are worn out.)

Urgence - Emergency.

Example: "C'est une urgence." (It's an emergency.)

Urbain - Urban.

Example: "Il vit dans un milieu urbain." (He lives in an urban environment.)

Usurpateur - Impostor.

Example: "C'est un usurpateur." (He's an impostor.)

Utile - Useful.

Example: "C'est un outil utile." (It's a useful tool.)

Ultra - Ultra, extreme.

Example: "C'est un ultra de ce groupe." (He's an extreme fan of this group.)

Uni - Plain, solid-colored.

Example: "Ce tissu est uni." (This fabric is plain.)

Usage - Usage, use.

Example: "L'usage de ce mot est courant." (The usage of this word is common.)

Universel - Universal.

Example: "C'est une règle universelle." (It's a universal rule.)

Ustensile - Utensil.

Example: "Prends cet ustensile." (Take this utensil.)

Ulcère - Ulcer.

Example: "Il a un ulcère à l'estomac." (He has a stomach ulcer.)

Unanime - Unanimous.

Example: "La décision était unanime." (The decision was unanimous.)

Usine - Factory.

Example: "Il travaille dans une usine." (He works in a factory.)

Urbain - Polished, suave.

Example: "Il a un air urbain." (He has a suave air.)

Utilitaire - Utility vehicle.

Example: "Il conduit un utilitaire." (He drives a utility vehicle.)

Ultime - Ultimate, final.

Example: "C'est son ultime chance." (It's his final chance.)

Usité - Commonly used.

Example: "Ce mot est très usité." (This word is very commonly used.)

Ultraviolet - Ultraviolet.

Example: "Les rayons ultraviolets sont dangereux." (Ultraviolet rays are dangerous.)

Urbain - Civil, courteous.

Example: "Il est très urbain." (He's very courteous.)

Usurpation - Impersonation, fraud.

Example: "Il a été accusé d'usurpation d'identité." (He was accused of identity fraud.)

V

Vachement - Really.

Example: "C'est vachement bien!" (It's really good!)

Vas-y - Go ahead.

Example: "Vas-y, essaie!" (Go ahead, try it!)

Vénère - Annoyed.

Example: "Je suis vénère." (I'm annoyed.)

Vieille - Old lady.

Example: "Il aide une vieille dame." (He's helping an old lady.)

Virer - To fire, to turn.

Example: "Il a été viré." (He was fired.)

Vive - Hooray.

Example: "Vive la France!" (Hooray for France!)

Vanner - To tease.

Example: "Il n'arrête pas de me vanner." (He keeps teasing me.)

Vieillir - To age.

Example: "Il vieillit bien." (He's aging well.)

Vachement - Extremely.

Example: "C'est vachement cool." (It's extremely cool.)

Vautour - Vulture.

Example: "Il ressemble à un vautour." (He looks like a vulture.)

Velours - Velvet.

Example: "Ce tissu est en velours." (This fabric is velvet.)

Vlan - Bang, whack.

Example: "Et vlan, il a frappé la table." (And bang, he hit the table.)

Vanne - Joke, dig.

Example: "Il m'a fait une vanne." (He made a joke at my expense.)

Verdure - Greenery.

Example: "J'aime la verdure de ce parc." (I love the greenery in this park.)

Vacherie - Dirty trick.

Example: "C'est une vraie vacherie." (That's a real dirty trick.)

Vantard - Boaster.

Example: "Il est trop vantard." (He's too boastful.)

Vider - To empty.

Example: "Il a vidé son sac." (He emptied his bag.)

Vif - Lively, quick.

Example: "Il est très vif." (He's very quick.)

Vigile - Security guard.

Example: "Le vigile est à l'entrée." (The security guard is at the entrance.)

Vie - Life.

Example: "La vie est belle." (Life is beautiful.)

W

Week-end - Weekend.

Example: "On se voit ce week-end." (We'll see each other this weekend.)

Whisky - Whiskey.

Example: "Il boit du whisky." (He drinks whiskey.)

Wagon - Train car.

Example: "Nous sommes dans le wagon numéro 3." (We're in car number 3.)

Wi-fi - Wireless internet.

Example: "Il y a du wi-fi ici." (There's wi-fi here.)

Web - Internet.

Example: "Il navigue sur le web." (He's surfing the web.)

Western - Western movie.

Example: "Il regarde un western." (He's watching a western.)

Wasabi - Spicy Japanese condiment.

Example: "Le wasabi est très piquant." (Wasabi is very spicy.)

Wagon-lit - Sleeping car.

Example: "Nous avons réservé un wagon-lit." (We reserved a sleeping car.)

Water-polo - Water polo.

Example: "Il joue au water-polo." (He plays water polo.)

Walkman - Portable music player.

Example: "Il écoute de la musique avec son walkman." (He listens to music with his walkman.)

Win - To win.

Example: "Il veut win la compétition." (He wants to win the competition.)

Warrant - Stock option.

Example: "Il a des warrants dans son portefeuille." (He has stock options in his portfolio.)

Windsurf - Wind surfing.

Example: "Ils font du windsurf." (They are windsurfing.)

Wesh - Hey, yo.

Example: "Wesh, ça va?" (Hey, how's it going?)

Webcam - Webcam.

Example: "Il a une webcam sur son ordinateur." (He has a webcam on his computer.)

Whisky-coca - Whiskey and coke.

Example: "Je prends un whisky-coca." (I'll have a whiskey and coke.

Wapiti - Elk.

Example: "Le wapiti est un grand cervidé." (The wapiti is a large deer.

Wifi - Wireless internet.

Example: "Il y a du wifi gratuit." (There's free wifi.)

Washington - Capital of the USA.

Example: "Il vit à Washington." (He lives in Washington.)

Wombat - Australian marsupial.

Example: "Le wombat est un animal australien." (The wombat is an Australian animal.)

X

Xénophobe - Xenophobic.

Example: "Il a des idées xénophobes." (He has xenophobic ideas.)

Xéroxer - To photocopy.

Example: "Il faut xéroxer ce document." (We need to photocopy this document.)

Xylophone - Musical instrument.

Example: "Il joue du xylophone." (He plays the xylophone.)

Xylophage - Wood-eating.

Example: "Les termites sont xylophages." (Termites are wood-eating.)

X - Used to replace letters in censored words.

Example: "C'est de la mde!" (It's st!)

Xiphoïde - Sword-shaped.

Example: "L'appendice xiphoïde est une partie du sternum." (The xiphoid process is part of the sternum.)

Xénon - Chemical element.

Example: "Le xénon est utilisé dans les lampes." (Xenon is used in lamps.)

Xérès - Sherry wine.

Example: "Il boit du xérès." (He drinks sherry.)

Xénogreffe - Transplant from another species.

Example: "La xénogreffe est encore expérimentale." (Xenotransplantation is still experimental.)

Xylophagie - Eating wood.

Example: "La xylophagie est courante chez certains insectes." (Wood-eating is common among certain insects.)

Xylotome - Tool for cutting wood.

Example: "Il utilise un xylotome." (He uses a tool for cutting wood.)

Xylophage - Insect that eats wood.

Example: "Les xylophages détruisent les meubles en bois." (Wood-eating insects destroy wooden furniture.)

Xénophilie - Love for foreign things.

Example: "Sa xénophilie est évidente." (His love for foreign things is evident.)

Xylème - Tissue in vascular plants.

Example: "Le xylème transporte l'eau dans les plantes." (Xylem transports water in plants.)

Xanthophile - Lover of yellow.

Example: "Elle est xanthophile." (She loves yellow.)

Xérophile - Plant that thrives in dry conditions.

Example: "Le cactus est xérophile." (The cactus is a xérophile.)

Xéranthème - Dried flower.

Example: "Elle a un bouquet de xéranthèmes." (She has a bouquet of dried flowers.)

Xérorésistant - Resistant to dryness.

Example: "Cette plante est xérorésistante." (This plant is resistant to dryness.)

Xénonarcose - Anesthesia using xenon.

Example: "La xénonarcose est une méthode d'anesthésie." (Xenon anesthesia is a method of anesthesia.)

Xénobiotique - Foreign chemical substance in an organism.

Example: "Le corps élimine les xénobiotiques." (The body eliminates foreign chemical substances.)

Y

Youpi - Yay, hooray.

Example: "Youpi, c'est les vacances!" (Yay, it's vacation time!)

Yoyo - Ups and downs.

Example: "Son humeur fait des yoyos." (His mood goes up and down.)

Yen - Yearning, desire.

Example: "Il a le yen de partir." (He has the desire to leave.)

Yacht - Yacht.

Example: "Ils naviguent en yacht." (They are sailing in a yacht.)

YouTube - Popular video-sharing website.

Example: "Je regarde des vidéos sur YouTube." (I watch videos on YouTube.)

Yougoslave - Yugoslavian.

Example: "Il est yougoslave." (He's Yugoslavian.)

Yankee - American (informal).

Example: "Il est un vrai yankee." (He's a real American.)

Yogi - Practitioner of yoga.

Example: "Elle est une yogi." (She is a yoga practitioner.)

Yeux - Eyes.

Example: "Elle a de beaux yeux." (She has beautiful eyes.)

Yodel - Yodel (singing style).

Example: "Il sait yodeler." (He knows how to yodel.)

Yuzu - Japanese citrus fruit.

Example: "Le yuzu est un agrume japonais." (Yuzu is a Japanese citrus fruit.)

Yéyé - Style of French pop music from the 1960s.

Example: "La musique yéyé est très populaire." (Yéyé music is very popular.)

Yahoo - Exclamation of joy.

Example: "Yahoo, on a gagné!" (Yahoo, we won!)

Yogi - Practitioner of yoga.

Example: "Il est un yogi expérimenté." (He is an experienced yoga practitioner.)

Youpala - Baby walker.

Example: "Le bébé joue dans son youpala." (The baby is playing in his walker.)

Yeniche - European nomadic group.

Example: "Les Yéniches voyagent à travers l'Europe." (The Yeniche people travel across Europe.)

Youyou - Small boat.

Example: "Ils rament dans un youyou." (They are rowing in a small boat.)

Yeti - Mythical creature.

Example: "Ils cherchent le yéti dans les montagnes." (They are searching for the yeti in the mountains.)

Yaourt - Yogurt.

Example: "Il mange un yaourt." (He's eating yogurt.)

Yersinia - Genus of bacteria.

Example: "La bactérie Yersinia est responsable de la peste." (The Yersinia bacterium is responsible for the plague.)

Z

Zut - Darn, damn.

Example: "Zut, j'ai oublié mes clés!" (Darn, I forgot my keys!)

Zéro - Zero, loser.

Example: "C'est un zéro." (He's a loser.)

Zapper - To change channels.

Example: "Il zappe tout le temps." (He changes channels all the time.)

Zénith - Peak, zenith.

Example: "Il est au zénith de sa carrière." (He is at the peak of his career.)

Zizanie - Discord, trouble.

Example: "Il sème la zizanie." (He is sowing discord.)

Zouk - Caribbean dance music.

Example: "Ils dansent le zouk." (They are dancing zouk.)

Zigzag - To zigzag.

Example: "Il marche en zigzag." (He is walking in a zigzag.)

Zibeline - Sable (animal).

Example: "La zibeline est un animal précieux." (The sable is a valuable animal.)

Zélateur - Zealot.

Example: "Il est un zélateur fervent." (He is a fervent zealot.)

Zébu - Zebu (type of cattle).

Example: "Le zébu est un animal d'Asie." (The zebu is an animal from Asia.)

Zodiaque - Zodiac.

Example: "Elle connaît bien le zodiaque." (She knows the zodiac well.)

Zyeuter - To peek.

Example: "Il zyeute par la fenêtre." (He is peeking through the window.)

Zénophobe - Fear of gods.

Example: "Il souffre de zénophobie." (He suffers from fear of gods.)

Zinzolin - Reddish-purple color.

Example: "Elle porte une robe zinzoline." (She is wearing a reddish-purple dress.)

Zoologie - Study of animals.

Example: "Elle étudie la zoologie." (She is studying zoology.)

Zéroïte - Materialist.

Example: "Il est très zéroïte." (He is very materialistic.)

Zélateur - Follower.

Example: "Il est un zélateur dévoué." (He is a devoted follower.)

Zénon - Greek philosopher.

Example: "Zénon est connu pour ses paradoxes." (Zeno is known for his paradoxes.)

Zénitude - Calmness.

Example: "Elle pratique la zénitude." (She practices calmness.)

Zézayer - To lisp.

Example: "Il zézaye légèrement." (He lisps slightly.)

Printed in Great Britain
by Amazon